Baby Bears

Bobbie Kalman

Crabtree Publishing Company
www.crabtreebooks.com

D1444765

It's fun to learn about Baby Animals

Created by Bobbie Kalman

For Charlie, our little baby bear,
with love from Grandpa Peter and Grandma Bobbie

Author and Editor-in-Chief
Bobbie Kalman

Editor
Robin Johnson

Text and Photo Research
Crystal Sikkens

Design
Katherine Berti
Samantha Crabtree (cover)

Production coordinator
Katherine Berti

Illustrations
Barbara Bedell: page 18
Tammy Everts: page 16
Barb Hinterhoeller: page 21 (bottom)
Katherine Berti: pages 9, 24 (vertebrates)
Bonna Rouse: pages 21 (top), 22, 24 (dens and life cycle)
Margaret Amy Salter: page 5

Photographs
© Bruce Coleman Inc.: Leonard L. Rue III: page 4 (bottom)
© iStockphoto.com: pages 5, 6 (bottom), 7, 8, 17 (right),
    19 (top), 20
© 2008 Jupiterimages Corporation: page 12
© Shutterstock.com: cover, pages 1, 4 (top), 6 (top left and
    right), 9, 10, 11, 13 (bottom), 15 (top), 16, 17 (left), 23,
    24 (all except mothers and polar bears)
© Michelle Vipond, www.sxc.hu: page 14
Other images by Corbis, Creatas, and Photodisc

Library and Archives Canada Cataloguing in Publication

Kalman, Bobbie, 1947-
    Baby bears / Bobbie Kalman.

(It's fun to learn about baby animals)
Includes index.
ISBN 978-0-7787-3968-5 (pbk.).--ISBN 978-0-7787-3949-4 (bound)

    1. Bears--Infancy--Juvenile literature. I. Title. II. Series.

QL737.C27K34 2008   j599.78'139   C2008-900141-9

Library of Congress Cataloging-in-Publication Data

Kalman, Bobbie.
    Baby bears / Bobbie Kalman.
        p. cm. -- (It's fun to learn about baby animals)
    Includes index.
    ISBN-13: 978-0-7787-3968-5 (pbk. : alk. paper)
    ISBN-13: 978-0-7787-3949-4 (library binding : alk. paper)
    ISBN-10: 0-7787-3968-6 (pbk. : alk. paper)
    ISBN-10: 0-7787-3949-X (library binding : alk. paper)
    1. Bear cubs--Juvenile literature. 2. Bears--Juvenile literature. I. Title. II. Series.

QL737.C27K349 2008
599.78'139--dc22
                                        2007052902

Crabtree Publishing Company

www.crabtreebooks.com   1-800-387-7650

Printed in Canada/042018/MQ20180319

Published in Canada
Crabtree Publishing
616 Welland Ave.
St. Catharines, Ontario
L2M 5V6

Published in the United States
Crabtree Publishing
PMB 59051
350 Fifth Avenue, 59th Floor
New York, New York 10118

Published in the United Kingdom
Crabtree Publishing
Maritime House
Basin Road North, Hove
BN41 1WR

Published in Australia
Crabtree Publishing
3 Charles Street
Coburg North
VIC, 3058

What is in this book?

What is a bear?

Bears are animals called **mammals**. Mammals have hair or fur on their bodies. Bears are covered with fur. Mammals are born. You were born, too. You are a mammal.

*Baby bears are called **cubs**. Cubs are born with their eyes shut. Their eyes open when they are about six weeks old. This brown bear cub was just born. It has very little fur.*

Mammal mothers make milk inside their bodies. Mammal babies **nurse** from their mothers. To nurse is to drink mother's milk.

These polar bear cubs are nursing.

Kinds of bears

There are eight kinds of bears. The bears shown on this page are an American black bear, a brown bear, and a polar bear. These bears all live in North America.

American black bears can be different colors. What color is this black bear?

There are different kinds of brown bears. This grizzly bear is one kind of brown bear.

Polar bears have white fur. They live in a cold place called the Arctic.

People who study bears once thought that giant pandas were raccoons. Now people think that these animals are bears. There are not many giant pandas left in the world. Giant pandas live in China.

Bear bodies

Bears have four legs. They can walk on all four legs or on their two back legs. They have five toes with **claws** on each foot. Claws are curved nails.

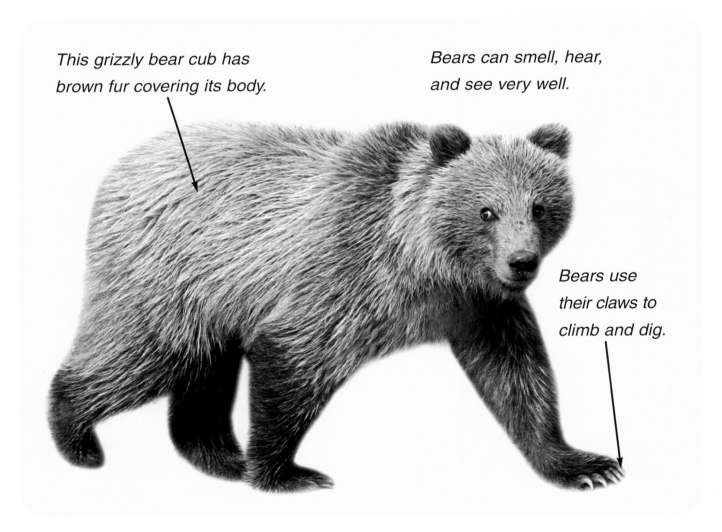

This grizzly bear cub has brown fur covering its body.

Bears can smell, hear, and see very well.

Bears use their claws to climb and dig.

Bears are **vertebrates**. Vertebrates are animals with **backbones**. A backbone is a row of bones down the middle of an animal's back. All the bones in an animal's body make up its **skeleton**.

This drawing shows a bear's skeleton. A skeleton holds an animal's body together.

backbone

This black bear cub is walking on four legs.

This black bear cub is standing on two legs.

9

Bear coats

Bears have two kinds of fur. Some of their fur is short, and some is long. Their short fur keeps them warm. Their long fur keeps water away from their skin. These bear cubs are called black bears, but they are not black. What colors are their coats?

panda cub

polar bear cub

Pandas have black-and-white fur. They have black fur around their eyes, ears, legs, and shoulders. Polar bears have thick white fur. Their skin is black. You can see the black skin on this cub's chin.

Bear families

A bear family is made up of a mother bear and her cubs. Most mother bears have **litters** of cubs. A litter is two or more babies that are born at the same time. This mother grizzly bear has three cubs.

Mother bears take good care of their cubs. They **groom** the cubs, or keep them clean.

A mother panda has only one baby at a time.

Learn from Mom!

Cubs stay with their mothers until they are two to three years old. They watch their mothers to learn how to live on their own. Mother bears teach their cubs where to find food and how to stay safe.

This mother bear is teaching her cubs how to climb a tree. Bear cubs need to climb trees to get away from animals that could hurt them.

This mother brown bear is teaching her cub how to catch fish.

These polar bear cubs are learning how to swim.

What do bears eat?

Most bears are **omnivores**. Omnivores are animals that eat both plants and animals. Bears eat honey, berries, leaves, and eggs. They also eat insects, fish, and other animals. Polar bears are **carnivores**. Carnivores eat mainly other animals. Pandas are **herbivores**. Herbivores eat mainly plants.

Pandas eat plants called bamboo.

This brown bear cub has caught a salmon to eat. Brown bears love salmon!

This black bear is climbing a tree to get some leaves to eat.

Bear habitats

Bears live in different places. The natural place where a bear lives is called its **habitat**. Many bears live in **forests**. Forests are habitats with many trees. Some bears live on mountains. Pandas live in forests that grow high on mountains. Bamboo grows in these forests.

These polar bears are keeping one another warm in their cold Arctic habitat.

Black bears live in forests across North America. They find many plants to eat in forests.

Winter sleep

Some bears live in places that have cold winters. It is hard for the bears to find food when it is cold. To stay alive, they sleep through most of the winter. During the summer and fall, the bears eat a lot of food. They store the food as **fat** on their bodies. The bears live off the fat during the winter.

These grizzly bears are eating a lot of salmon. They are getting ready for winter.

Mother bears that live in cold places have their cubs in winter. Before the cubs are born, the mother builds a home called a **den**. The den is a warm and safe place for the bears to live. After the cubs are born, the mother goes to sleep. The cubs nurse while their mother sleeps.

Many bears make their dens by digging holes in hills or under tree roots. Some bears use caves or holes in logs for their dens.

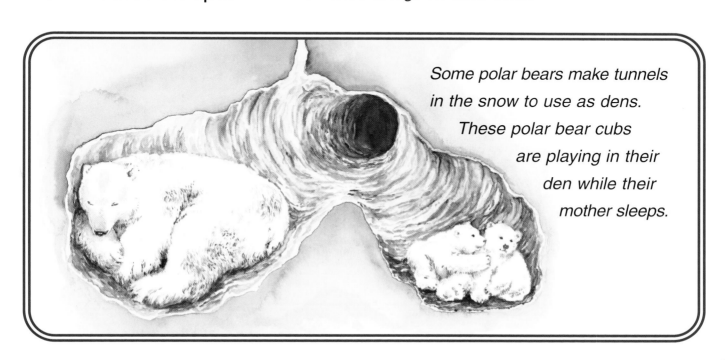

Some polar bears make tunnels in the snow to use as dens. These polar bear cubs are playing in their den while their mother sleeps.

Cubs grow up

Each bear goes through a set of changes called a **life cycle**. A life cycle starts when a cub is born. The cub grows and changes. It then becomes an adult bear. These pictures show the life cycle of an American black bear.

Adult bears can make babies.

A black bear cub drinks its mother's milk.

The cub becomes an adult when it is three to five years old.

Soon the cub leaves the den. It still nurses, but it starts eating other foods, too.

This black bear cub has just left its den. It is starting to learn about the world. The cub will quickly find out why it should not play with skunks!

This mother bear and her cubs are looking for food in a forest. The cubs will soon start living on their own and finding food for themselves.

Words to Know and Index

black bears
pages 6, 9, 10, 17, 19, 22, 23

grizzly bear

brown bears
pages 4, 6, 8, 12, 15, 17, 20

dens
pages 21, 22, 23

food
pages 14, 16-17, 20, 22, 23

fur
pages 4, 6, 8, 10-11

habitats
pages 18-19

life cycle
pages 22-23

mothers
pages 5, 12, 13, 14, 15, 21, 22, 23

pandas
pages 7, 11, 13, 16, 18

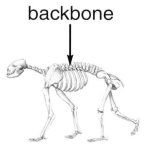

polar bears
pages 5, 6, 11, 15, 16, 19, 21

backbone

vertebrates
page 9

24